PREFACE

We are pleased to present the CBSE Data Science Class 12 Solved Papers for the academic years, compiled under subject code 844. This book is designed to be an invaluable resource for students preparing for their board exams, offering a collection of actual CBSE exam papers along with detailed solutions crafted by subject matter experts.
As Data Science continues to evolve as a critical field of study, it demands not only a strong grasp of theoretical concepts but also the ability to apply this knowledge in practical scenarios. This book aims to bridge the gap between theory and practice by providing students with real exam questions and step-by-step solutions that align with the CBSE marking scheme.

Key Features of This Book:
Authentic Exam Papers: The book includes the exact question papers from the CBSE board exams of 2023 and 2024, ensuring that students have access to the most current and relevant material.
Comprehensive Solutions: Each question is solved in detail, providing clear explanations and guiding students on how to approach different types of problems effectively.
Marking Scheme Insights: Solutions are aligned with the official CBSE marking scheme, offering students a clear understanding of how marks are allocated, which helps them focus on key areas to maximize their scores.
Exam Strategy and Tips: The book includes strategic advice on time management, common mistakes to avoid, and tips on how to present answers to score higher marks.
Thorough Syllabus Coverage: Every major topic within the Data Science syllabus is covered, making this book a comprehensive tool for exam preparation.

This collection of solved papers is intended to serve as both a practice tool and a guide for students aiming to achieve excellence in their CBSE Data Science exams. By working through these papers, students will not only enhance their understanding of the subject but also gain the confidence needed to excel in the examination hall.

We hope this book will be an essential companion in your journey toward academic success, providing you with the tools and insights necessary to master the subject of Data Science.
We wish all students the very best in their preparations and in their forthcoming exams.

We believe that this book will be an invaluable resource for Class 12 students as they prepare for their Data Science board exams. By diligently working through these unsolved papers, students will not only improve their exam performance but also deepen their understanding of Data Science, laying a strong foundation for future studies and careers in this rapidly evolving field. We wish all students the best of luck in their exams and hope that this book serves as a crucial tool in their academic journey.

Table of Contents

CBSE Previous Year Question Paper 2023

SET-4

SUBJECT CODE: 844

Q.P. CODE: 368

Instructions:

Please check that this question paper contains **21** questions.

Q.P. Code given on the right-hand side of the question paper should be written on the title page of the answer-book by the candidate.

Please write down the serial number of the question in the answer-book before attempting it.

15-minute time has been allotted to read this question paper. The question paper will be distributed at 10.15 a.m. From 10.15 a.m. to 10.30 a.m., the students will read the question paper only and will not write any answer on the answer-book during this period.

DATA SCIENCE

Time allowed: 2 hours

Maximum Marks: 50

General Instructions:

1. Please read the instructions carefully.
2. This question paper consists of 21 questions in two sections: Section A and Section B.
3. Section A has Objective Type Questions, whereas Section B contains Subjective Type Questions.
4. Out of the given (5 + 16 =) 21 questions, the candidate has to answer (5 + 10 =) 15 questions in the allotted (maximum) time of 2 hours.
5. All questions of a particular section must be attempted in the correct order.
6. Section A: Objective Type Questions (24 marks):
    a. This section has 5 questions.
    b. There is no negative marking.
    c. Do as per the instructions given.
    d. Marks allotted are mentioned against each question/part.
7. Section B: Subjective Type Questions (26 marks):
    a. This section has 16 questions.
    b. A candidate has to do 10 questions.
    c. Do as per the instructions given.

d. Marks allotted are mentioned against each question/part.

SECTION A

(Objective Type Questions) (24 marks)

1. Answer any 4 out of the given 6 questions on Employability Skills. (4X1=4)

(i) A/An ________ may be defined as underlying characteristic of a person which results in effective and/or superior performance in a job.

(a) uncertainty

(b) competence

(c) obstacles

(d) fear

Answer: b

Reason: Competence refers to the skills, knowledge, and abilities that enable a person to perform tasks effectively and achieve superior performance in a job.

(ii) Which of the following is not true for formulas in a spreadsheet?

(a) A formula always starts with an equal to (=) sign.

(b) A formula is displayed in the formula bar.

(c) Formulae are used to calculate results through arithmetic operations

(d) In numeric formulae, you cannot make use of operators.

Answer: d

Reason: This statement is incorrect because in numeric formulas, operators such as +, -, *, and / are commonly used to perform arithmetic operations.

(iii) Given below are two statements, one labelled as Assertion (A) and the other labelled as Reason (R). Select the correct answer from the code given below:

Assertion (A): Physiological motivation can be guided by the need for achievement and the need for affiliation.

Reason (R): The need for achievement is a social form of motivation involving a competitive drive to meet the standards of excellence.

Code:

(a) Both Assertion (A) and Reason (R) are true and Reason (R) is the correct explanation of Assertion (A).

(b) Both Assertion (A) and Reason (R) are true, but Reason (R) is not the correct explanation of Assertion (A).

(c) Assertion (A) is true, but Reason (R) is false.

(d)Assertion (A) is false, but Reason (R) is true.

Answer: d

Reason: The need for achievement and the need for affiliation are psychological motivations, not physiological. However, Reason (R) correctly describes the need for achievement as a social form of motivation.

(iv) If the column is not wide enough to display the value, which of the following errors is displayed?

(a) #VALUE!

(b) #DIV/0!

(c) #####

(d) #COLUMN!

Answer: c

Reason: The "#####" error occurs in spreadsheets like Excel when the column width is insufficient to display the value, indicating that the column needs to be widened.

(v) Which term is used to describe a person's ability to recognize what results are important and the steps needed to be taken to achieve them?

(a) Motivation

(b) Result Orientation

(c) Stress Management

(d) Goal Setting

Answer: b

Reason: Result orientation refers to the ability to focus on the desired outcomes and to plan and execute the steps necessary to achieve those outcomes.

(vi) Given below are two statements, one labelled as Assertion (A) and the other labelled as Reason (R). Select the correct answer from the code given below:

Assertion (A): Many entrepreneurs are not considered experts in their line of business, but still they make important decisions and solve issues everyday within their industry.

Reason (R): By preparing oneself to take on the challenge and by taking smaller steps to work towards it, fearful situations can also start to feel comfortable.

Code:

(a) Both Assertion (A) and Reason (R) are true and Reason (R) is the correct explanation of Assertion (A).

(b) Both Assertion (A) and Reason (R) are true, but Reason (R) is not the correct explanation of Assertion (A).

(c) Assertion (A) is true, but Reason (R) is false.

(d) Assertion (A) is false, but Reason (R) is true.

Answer: b

Reason: While both statements are true individually, Reason (R) does not directly explain Assertion (A). Entrepreneurs may not be experts but can still make important decisions due to experience and adaptability, not necessarily due to overcoming fear in small steps.

2. Answer any 5 out of the given 6 questions. (5X1=5)

(i) ____________ is the right of an individual to have control over how his or her personal information is collected and used.

(a) Data Privacy

(b) Data Governance

(c) Governing

(d) Data Quality

Answer: (a) Data Privacy.

Reason: Data privacy is about an individual's right to control how their personal information is collected and used.

(ii) Which of the following refers to the process of identifying incorrect, incomplete and inaccurate data?

(a) Exploratory Data Analysis

(b) Data Cleaning

(c) Univariate Analysis

(d) Data Ethics

Answer: (b) Data Cleaning.

Reason: Data cleaning refers to the process of identifying and correcting incorrect, incomplete, and inaccurate data. It involves removing errors and inconsistencies to improve the quality of the data, making it more accurate and reliable for analysis.

(iii) Every ______________represents the outcome of the test in a decision tree.

(a) Internal node

(b) External node

(c) Branch

(d) Leaf node

Answer: (d) Leaf node.

Reason: In a decision tree, a leaf node represents the outcome or final decision of the test after traversing through the tree. Each path from the root node to a leaf node represents a classification or decision rule.

(iv) The ________ algorithm is one of the most basic and easy-to-implement supervised machine learning algorithms.

(a) Decision tree

(b) K-nearest neighbours (K-NN)

(c) Classification

(d) Scoping

Answer: (b) K-nearest neighbours (K-NN).

Reason: K-NN is a simple and easy-to-implement supervised machine learning algorithm that classifies data points based on the closest neighbours.

(v)___________ is the square root of the variance of the residuals.

(a) Root Mean Square Deviation

(b) Required Mean Similar Deviation

(c) Root Median Similar Deviation

(d) Regular Mean Square Deviation

Answer: (a) Root Mean Square Deviation.

Reason: The Root Mean Square Deviation (RMSD) is the square root of the variance of the residuals, which are the differences between observed and predicted values. RMSD provides a measure of the average magnitude of the residuals, giving insight into the accuracy of a model's predictions.

(vi) In which type of learning do algorithms act on data without human intervention?

(a) Unsupervised

(b) Supervised

(c) Limited

(d) Conditional

Answer: (a) Unsupervised.

Reason: In unsupervised learning, algorithms act on data without human intervention, meaning they are not provided with labelled outcomes or guidance. The algorithm identifies patterns and relationships within the data on its own, often used for clustering or association tasks.

3. Answer any 5 out of the given 6 questions. (5X1=5)

(i) PDP stands for

(a) Personal Data Protection Bill

(b) Private Data Protection Bill

(c) Personal Device Protection Bill

(d) Personal Device Prevention Bill

Answer: (a) Personal Data Protection Bill.

Reason: PDP stands for Personal Data Protection Bill, which is a proposed law in some countries that aims to protect individuals' personal data by regulating how it is collected, stored, and used. It is designed to ensure data privacy and security.

(ii) _________is a more complex form of statistical analysis technique and is used to analyse more than two variables in the data set.

(a) Graphical method

(b) Multivariate analysis

(c) Univariate analysis

(d) Unsupervised learning technique

Answer: (b) Multivariate analysis.

Reason: Multivariate analysis is a statistical technique used to analyse more than two variables simultaneously within a dataset. It allows researchers to understand relationships between multiple variables and is more complex compared to univariate or bivariate analysis, which deals with one or two variables respectively.

(iii) Decision trees are used to solve problems.

(a) Only classification

(b) Only regression

(c) Both classification and regression

(d) All universal

Answer: (c) Both classification and regression.

Reason: Decision trees can be used to solve both classification and regression problems. For classification, decision trees help in categorizing data into discrete classes. For regression, they are used to predict continuous values.

(iv) Can we use K-NN algorithms for data mining problems?

Answer: Yes, K-NN algorithms can be used for data mining problems.

Reason: K-NN (K-Nearest Neighbors) is a versatile algorithm commonly used in data mining for tasks such as classification, regression, and pattern recognition. It is particularly effective in scenarios where you want to categorize or predict outcomes based on the similarity to known data points. Because K-NN is non-parametric and easy to implement, it is widely used in various data mining applications.

(v) $Y = m \quad X + b$ is the formula for __________.

(a) Mean Absolute Error

(b) Root Mean Square Deviation

(c) Simple linear regression

(d) Simple linear classification

Answer: (c) Simple linear regression.

Reason: The formula $Y=m \cdot X+bY$ represents a simple linear regression, where Y is the dependent variable, X is the independent variable, m is the slope of the line, and b is the y-intercept. This equation models the relationship between two variables with a straight line.

(vi) State whether the following statement is true or false:

The formula for non-linear and linear regression is same.

Answer: False.

Reason: Linear and non-linear regressions have different formulas because they model different types of relationships between variables.

4. Answer any 5 out of the given 6 questions. **(5X1=5)**

(i) The Children's Online Privacy and Protection Act is a law that deals with

(a) privacy policy for children who are less than the age of 13 years.

(b) privacy policy for adults.

(c) public policy for all children.

(d) protection policy for mothers of newborns.

Answer: (a) Privacy policy for children who are less than the age of 13 years.

Reason: COPPA protects the privacy of children under 13 by regulating how their information is collected and used online.

(ii) The process of Exploratory Data Analysis is done with the help of summary statistics and representations.

(a) Analytical

(b) Graphical

(c) Logical

(d) Sequential

Answer: (b) Graphical.

Reason: Exploratory Data Analysis (EDA) involves using summary statistics and graphical representations, such as histograms, box plots, and scatter plots, to explore and understand the data's patterns, trends, and relationships.

(iii) Regression trees are used when the dependent variable is non-continuous. Is the given statement true or false?

Answer: False.

Reason: Regression trees are used when the dependent variable is continuous, not non-continuous. They are designed to predict a continuous outcome, making them suitable for regression tasks rather than classification tasks.

(iv) Which of the following is true for K-NN algorithm?

(a) Interpretability of the K-NN algorithm is very low.

(b) The K-NN algorithm explicitly has a training step.

(c) The K-NN algorithm is not sensitive to outliers.

(d) K-NN works well with a small number of input variables, but as the number of variables grow, the K-NN algorithm struggles to predict the output of a new data point.

Answer: (d) K-NN works well with a small number of input variables, but struggles as the number of variables grows.

Reason: K-NN faces challenges in high-dimensional spaces due to the "curse of dimensionality," making predictions less accurate.

(v) The actual value of the ________depends on the data and accuracy required.

(a) RMSE

(b) MAE

(c) NLR

(d) model

Answer: (a) RMSE.

Reason: The actual value of the Root Mean Square Error (RMSE) depends on the data and the level of accuracy required. RMSE is a measure of the differences between predicted and observed values, and it varies based on the specific data set and the precision needed for the model's predictions.

(vi) Trigonometric functions are examples of linear functions.

Is the given statement true or false?

Answer: False.

Reason: Trigonometric functions (like sine, cosine, and tangent) are not linear functions. Linear functions have a constant rate of change and produce straight-line graphs, while trigonometric functions are periodic and produce wave-like curves, indicating they are non-linear.

5. Answer any 5 out of the given 6 questions. (5X1=5)

(i) Ethics govern the behaviour or actions of an individual.

(a) True

(b) False

Answer: (a) True

Reason: Ethics are principles that govern the behaviour or actions of individuals, guiding them to differentiate between right and wrong, and influencing their decisions and conduct in various situations.

(ii) Bivariate analysis is also a good way to measure the between the two variables.

(a) Difference

(b) Mean

(c) Correlation

(d) Median

Answer: (c) Correlation

Reason: Bivariate analysis measures the relationship between two variables, often assessing their correlation.

(iii) For every possible decision in a decision tree, stemming from the root makes a _________.

(a) Branch

(b) Tree

(c) Root

(d) Node

Answer: (a) Branch.

Reason: In a decision tree, each possible decision or choice stemming from the root node creates a branch. These branches represent the different paths that can be taken based on the decision rules applied at each node.

(iv) ___________ is a non-parametric algorithm, as it does not assume anything about the distribution of the data.

(a) Cross Validation

(b) Regression

(c) Dataset

(d) K-NN

Answer: (d) K-NN

Reason: K-NN is non-parametric because it makes no assumptions about the data's distribution.

(v) What is the basic objective of linear regression?

(a) To reduce the distance between the line and data points to make it minimum.

(b) To increase the distance between the line and data points to make it maximum.

(c) To find the sum of the distance between the line and data points.

(d) To find the average of the distance between the line and data points.

Answer: (a) To reduce the distance between the line and data points to make it minimum.

Reason: Linear regression aims to minimize the errors between the data points and the predicted line.

(vi) A _________ regression equation has an intercept on the right-hand side and an explanatory variable with a coefficient.

(a) circular

(b) multiple

(c) complex

(d) simple

Answer: (d) Simple

Reason: A simple regression equation includes an intercept and one explanatory variable with a coefficient.

SECTION B

(Subjective Type Questions) (26 marks)

Answer any 3 out of the given 5 questions on Employability Skills. Answer each question in 20 30 words. (3X2=6)

6. List any two benefits of Entrepreneurial Competencies.

Answer: Two benefits of Entrepreneurial Competencies are:

1. Enhanced Problem-Solving Ability: Entrepreneurial competencies enable individuals to effectively identify and analyse problems, leading to innovative and practical solutions that drive business success.
2. Increased Adaptability: These competencies help entrepreneurs quickly adapt to changing market conditions and unexpected challenges, ensuring the sustainability and growth of their business.

7. Answer the following questions from the spreadsheet given below:

My Store

My Store				
	A	B	C	D
1	Product	Cost Price	Selling Price	Profit/Loss
2	Ruler	9	15	
3	Crayons	23	25	
4	Pens	14	12	
5	Cardboard	35	45	
6	Highest			

a. Write a formula in cell D2, to calculate the Profit or Loss for the item 'Ruler' as the difference of "Cost Price" and "Selling Price".

b. Write a function in B6 to display the highest cost price of the product.

Answer:

a. The formula to calculate the profit or loss in cell D2 is: =C2-B2

b. The function to display the highest cost price in cell B6 is: =MAX (B2:B5)

8. List any two sources of motivation and inspiration.

Answer:

1. Personal Goals and Ambitions: Setting and striving to achieve personal goals can be a strong source of motivation,

driving individuals to work hard and stay focused.

2. Role Models and Mentors: Observing the success and guidance of role models or mentors can inspire and motivate individuals to pursue their own dreams and overcome challenges.

9. Differentiate between internal and external motivation. Give a suitable example.

Answer:

Internal Motivation:

Internal motivation comes from within an individual. It is driven by personal satisfaction, interest, or the desire to achieve a personal goal. For example, a student studying hard because they enjoy learning and want to master the subject is experiencing internal motivation.

External Motivation:

External motivation is influenced by external factors such as rewards, recognition, or the desire to avoid negative consequences. For example, a student working hard to get good grades to receive a reward from their parents is driven by external motivation.

10. Match the given attitudes of an entrepreneur with their characteristics:

Attitudes	Characteristics
e) Interpersonal skills	(vi) Ability to take charge and act in a (vii) situation before others
f) Taking initiative	(viii) Ability to continue to do something even when it is difficult.
g) Decisiveness	(ix) Ability to work with others
h) Perseverance	(x) Ability to make quick and profitable

Answer:

a) Interpersonal skills - (iv) Ability to work with others

b) Taking initiativc - (i) Ability to take charge and act in a situation before others

c) Decisiveness - (v) Ability to make quick and profitable decisions

d) Perseverance - (iii) Ability to continue to do something even when it is difficult

Answer any 4 out of the given 6 questions in 20 - 30 words each. **(4X2=8)**

11. Name the areas of focus of data governance.

Answer: Data governance focuses on areas such as data quality, data privacy, data security, data stewardship, data integration, data architecture, and compliance with regulations to ensure effective data management and usage.

12. Differentiate between Univariate analysis and Bivariate analysis.

Answer: Univariate analysis examines a single variable to summarize and describe its characteristics, while bivariate analysis explores the relationship between two variables, often measuring correlation or association.

13. Why are decision trees considered to be versatile?

Answer: Decision trees are considered versatile because they can handle both classification and regression tasks, work with various data types, and are easy to interpret, making them useful in diverse applications.

14. What is the principle on which K-NN algorithm work?

Answer: The K-NN algorithm works on the principle of proximity, classifying a data point based on the majority class of its nearest neighbors, assuming that similar points are close in feature space.

15. When do we use linear regression?

Answer: Linear regression is used when we want to model the relationship between a dependent variable and one or more independent variables, particularly when the relationship is assumed to be linear.

16. The formula for non-linear regression is $y \sim f(x, \beta)$.

What do x and y denote in the given formula?

Answer: In the formula $y \sim f(x,\beta)$ for non-linear regression, x denotes the independent variable(s) or predictor(s), and y represents the dependent variable or the outcome being predicted.

Answer any 3 out of the given 5 questions in 50 - 80 words each. **(3X4=12)**

17. Write a short note on General Data Protection Regulation (GDPR).

Answer: The General Data Protection Regulation (GDPR) is a comprehensive data protection law enacted by the European Union (EU) in May 2018. It aims to protect the privacy and personal data of EU citizens, regardless of where the data is processed. GDPR imposes strict rules on data handling, including obtaining explicit consent, ensuring data security, and providing individuals with the right to access, correct, and delete their data. Non-compliance can result in significant fines, making GDPR a critical regulation for organizations worldwide.

18. List any four tools and methods used to perform Exploratory Analysis.

Answer: Four common tools and methods used to perform Exploratory Data Analysis (EDA) are:

Summary Statistics: Calculating measures like mean, median, mode, and standard deviation to understand the central tendency and dispersion of data.

Data Visualization: Using plots such as histograms, box plots, and scatter plots to visually explore data patterns and distributions.

Correlation Analysis: Assessing the relationship between variables using correlation coefficients or heatmaps.

Data Cleaning: Identifying and handling missing values, outliers, and inconsistencies to improve data quality before further analysis.

19. List any four important features of decision trees.

Answer: Four important features of decision trees are:

1. Simplicity and Interpretability: Decision trees are easy to understand and interpret, as they visually represent decision paths.
2. Versatility: They can handle both classification and regression tasks, making them applicable in various scenarios.
3. Non-Parametric Nature: Decision trees do not assume any specific data distribution, allowing them to work with various types of data.
4. Handling of Categorical and Numerical Data: Decision trees can process both categorical and numerical variables, offering flexibility in data analysis.

20. List any four disadvantages of K-NN compared to other algorithms.

Answer: Four disadvantages of K-NN compared to other algorithms are:

1. Computational Complexity: K-NN can be slow, especially with large datasets, as it requires calculating the distance to every training point.
2. Sensitivity to Noise: K-NN is highly sensitive to noisy data and outliers, which can negatively impact accuracy.
3. Curse of Dimensionality: K-NN's performance deteriorates with an increasing number of features due to sparse data in high-dimensional spaces.
4. No Training Phase: K-NN lacks a training phase, making it inefficient in situations where rapid predictions are required.

21. Explain in points the working of 'k-means clustering algorithm'

Answer: Four disadvantages of K-NN compared to other algorithms are:

1. Computational Complexity: K-NN can be slow, especially with large datasets, as it requires calculating the distance to every training point.
2. Sensitivity to Noise: K-NN is highly sensitive to noisy data and outliers, which can negatively impact accuracy.
3. Curse of Dimensionality: K-NN's performance deteriorates with an increasing number of features due to sparse data in high-dimensional spaces.
4. No Training Phase: K-NN lacks a training phase, making it inefficient in situations where rapid predictions are required.

CBSE Previous Year Question Paper 2024

SET-4

SUBJECT CODE: 844

Q.P. CODE: 368

Instructions:

Please check that this question paper contains **21** questions.

Q.P. Code given on the right-hand side of the question paper should be written on the title page of the answer-book by the candidate.

Please write down the serial number of the question in the answer-book before attempting it. 15-minute time has been allotted to read this question paper. The question paper will be distributed at 10.15 a.m. From 10.15 a.m. to 10.30 a.m., the students will read the question paper only and will not write any answer on the answer-book during this period.

DATA SCIENCE

Time allowed: 2 hours **Maximum Marks: 50**

General Instructions:

1. Please read the instructions carefully.
2. This question paper consists of 21 questions in two sections: Section A and Section B.
3. Section A has Objective Type Questions, whereas Section B contains Subjective Type Questions.
4. Out of the given (5 + 16 =) 21 questions, the candidate has to answer (5 + 10 =) 15 questions in the allotted (maximum) time of 2 hours.
5. All questions of a particular section must be attempted in the correct order.
6. Section A: Objective Type Questions (24 marks):
   a. This section has 5 questions.
   b. There is no negative marking.
   c. Do as per the instructions given.
   d. Marks allotted are mentioned against each question/part.
7. Section B: Subjective Type Questions (26 marks):
   a. This section has 16 questions.
   b. A candidate has to do 10 questions.
   c. Do as per the instructions given.

d. Marks allotted are mentioned against each question/part.

SECTION A

(Objective Type Questions) (24 marks)

1. Answer any 4 out of the given 6 questions on Employability Skills. (4×1=4)

i) Match the following personalities with their parameters, based on Five Factor Model.

a. Extraversion	(i) Self-disciplined and take care of others before themselves.
b. Neuroticism	(ii) Talkative, confident, and make any gathering lively.
c. Consciousness	(iii) Self-doubt, depression and shyness.

(a) a- (ii), b - (iii), c- (i)

(b) a- (i), b- (ii), c- (iii)

(c) a- (iii), b- (ii), c- (i)

(d) a- (ii), b- (i), c- (iii)

Answer: d

Reason:

Extraversion is characterized by being talkative, confident, and lively in social situations, which matches option (ii).

Neuroticism involves emotional instability, leading to traits such as self-doubt, depression, and shyness, which matches option (iii).

Conscientiousness refers to being self-disciplined and having a strong sense of duty, often putting others' needs before their own, which aligns with option (i).

(ii) A _________ is a company that is in the first stage of its operations.

(a) Corporation

(b) Startup

(c) Multinational

(d) Conglomerate

Answer: b

Reason: A startup is a newly established company that is typically in the early stages of its operations, often focused on developing a unique product or service to bring to market.

(iii) Which non-verbal cue is not associated with active listening?

(a) Nodding in agreement

(b) Maintaining an open and welcoming body posture

(c) Checking your phone when the other person is speaking

(d) Making encouraging facial expressions

Answer: c

Reason: Active listening involves giving your full attention to the speaker. Checking your phone while someone is speaking is a distraction and shows disengagement, which is not a characteristic of active listening.

(iv) Statement (A): To sum the values in cells A1 through A10 in a spreadsheet, the formula used is "=SUM (A1:A10)".

Statement (A): To sum the values in cells A1 through A10 in a spreadsheet, the formula used is "=SUM (A1:A10)".

(a) Both (A) and (B) are true.

(b) Both (A) and (B) are false.

(c) (A) is true, but (B) is false.

(d) (A) is false, but (B) is true.

Answer: a

Reason: The formula "=SUM(A1)" is correctly used to sum the values in cells A1 through A10 in spreadsheet software like Microsoft Excel or Google Sheets.

(v) Why is setting SMART goals important in self-management?

(a) It makes goals too rigid.

(b) It allows for vague and undefined goals.

(c) It defines action-based steps that one will follow to achieve the goal.

(d) It discourages goal setting altogether.

Answer: c

Reason: SMART goals are Specific, Measurable, Achievable, Relevant, and Time-bound. They help in clearly defining the steps and actions needed to achieve a goal, making the process structured and manageable.

(vi) Which of the following is a benefit of green jobs?

(a) They do not support adaptation to climate change.

(b) They control waste and pollution.

(c) They increase greenhouse gas emissions.

(d) They decrease efficiency of raw materials.

Answer: b

Reason: Green jobs are aimed at reducing the environmental impact of industries by controlling waste and pollution, supporting sustainability, and helping adapt to climate change.

2. Answer any 5 out of the given 6 questions. (5×1=5)

(i) EDA stands for:

(a) Exploratory Data Analysis

(b) Efficient Data Accumulation

(c) Extended Data Assessment

(d) Essential Data Application

Answer: (a) Exploratory Data Analysis

Reason: EDA is the process of analysing data sets to summarize their main characteristics, often with visual methods.

(ii) Assertion (A): Decision trees are versatile algorithms and are easy to visualize.

Reasoning (R): Decision trees can only be used to map linear relationships.

(a) Both (A) and (R) are true and (R) is correct explanation of (A).

(b) Both (A) and (R) are true and (R) is not correct explanation of (A).

(c) (A) is true and (R) is false.

(d) (R) is true and (A) is false.

Answer: (c) (A) is true and (R) is false.

Reason: The assertion (A) that decision trees are versatile algorithms and easy to visualize is true. However, the reasoning (R) is false because decision trees can model both linear and non-linear relationships, not just linear ones. Therefore, (R) does not correctly explain (A).

(iii) Which of the following is not a focus area of data governance?

(a) Data integrity

(b) Data availability

(c) Usability of data

(d) Data visualization

Answer: (d) Data visualization

Reason: Data governance focuses on data integrity, availability, and usability, but data visualization is not a core focus area.

(iv) In the K-Nearest Neighbors (KNN) algorithm, what does the "K" represent?

(a) K is the number of training examples.

(b) K is the number of points that the K-NN algorithm checks before doing a majority vote.

(c) K is the number of points that the K-NN algorithm checks before doing a minority vote.

(d) K is the dimensionality of the data.

Answer: (b) K is the number of points that the K-NN algorithm checks before doing a majority vote.

Reason: In the K-Nearest Neighbors (KNN) algorithm, "K" represents the number of nearest data points considered when making a prediction. The algorithm checks these K points and then performs a majority vote among them to determine the classification of a new data point.

(v) Regression methods that do not have a linear function are called:

(a) Linear regression models

(b) Non-linear regression models

(c) Exponential regression models

(d) Polynomial regression models

Answer: (b) Non-linear regression models.

Reason: Regression methods that do not follow a linear relationship are referred to as non-linear regression models. These models capture more complex relationships between variables that cannot be adequately modeled by a straight line.

(vi) What is the primary characteristic of Multiple Linear Regression?

(a) It uses only one independent variable to predict the outcome of a dependent variable.

(b) It uses multiple dependent variables to predict the outcome of a single independent variable.

(c) It uses multiple independent variables to predict the outcome of a dependent variable.

(d) It employs categorical variables exclusively for prediction.

Answer: (c) It uses multiple independent variables to predict the outcome of a dependent variable.

Reason: Multiple Linear Regression involves predicting a dependent variable using multiple independent variables.

3. Answer any *5* out of the given *6* questions. *(5×1=5)*

(i) True or False: A company is collecting and storing personal identifiable information in a secure, encrypted format without obtaining explicit consent from the user. There is no agreement from the user regarding the collection of the data by the company. It is a clear violation of data privacy rules.

Answer: True.

Reason: Collecting personal data without user consent, even if encrypted, violates data privacy rules.

(ii) Statistical methods like mean, mode, median, range, variance and standard deviation are used for:

(a) Bivariate Analysis

(b) Multivariate Analysis

(c) Univariate Analysis

(d) Exponential Analysis

Answer: (c) Univariate Analysis.

Reason: Statistical methods like mean, mode, median, range, variance, and standard deviation are used in univariate analysis to summarize and describe the characteristics of a single variable.

(iii) When using a decision tree for classification, what does each leaf node represent?

(a) A subset of the dataset

(b) A class label

(c) A threshold value

(d) A continuous variable

Answer: (b) A class label.

Reason: In a decision tree used for classification, each leaf node represents a class label, which is the final outcome or category that the data point is classified into after traversing the tree.

(iv) What is the curse of dimensionality in the context of the K-Nearest Neighbors (KNN) algorithm?

(a) It refers to the phenomenon where KNN works well with a large number of input variables.

(b) It describes the ease with which KNN handles high- dimensional data.

(c) It suggests that KNN is not affected by the number of input variables.

(d) It explains that KNN works well with a small number of input variables but struggles as the number of variables grows.

Answer: The correct answer is (b) A class label.

Reason: In a classification decision tree, each leaf node represents the final decision or class label that the input data is assigned to after the tree's decisions have been made based on the features.

(v) The diagram below shows a scatter plot of two variables X and Y. Linear regression helps us to find Line X. What is Line X known as?

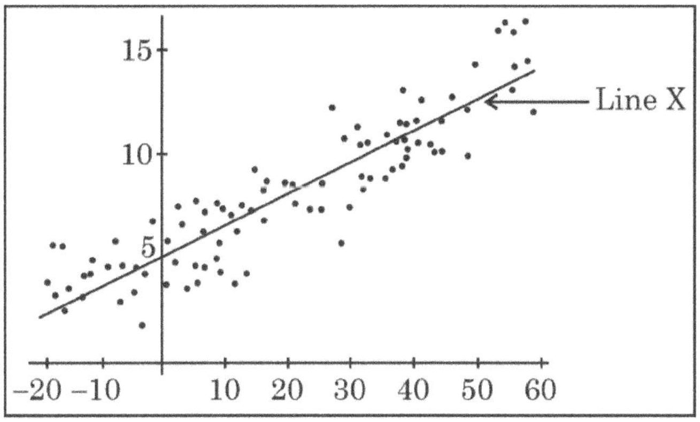

(a) Correlation line

(b) Line of best fit

(c) Regression line

(d) Trend line

Answer: (c) Regression line

Reason: The line in the scatter plot represents the best linear relationship between X and Y, known as the regression line.

(vi) What problem-solving approach does the K-Means clustering algorithm use?

(a) Gradient Descent

(b) Expectation-Maximization

(c) Principal Component Analysis (PCA)

(d) Genetic Algorithm

Answer: (b) Expectation-Maximization

Reason: K-Means clustering uses an approach similar to Expectation-Maximization, alternating between assigning points to clusters and updating centroids.

4. Answer any *5* out of the given *6* questions. **(5×*1*=*5*)**

(i) The European Union made protect European Union consumer data. effective on May 25th, 2018 to protect European Union consumer data.

(a) Health Insurance Portability and Accountability Act

(b) General Data Protection Regulation

(c) Personal Data Protection Bill

(d) California Consumer Privacy Act

Answer: (b) General Data Protection Regulation

Reason: GDPR is an EU law effective from May 25th, 2018, aimed at protecting EU citizens' personal data.

(ii) In a market survey we are analyzing the relationship between price and sales of a product to see if there is any relationship. This kind of analysis is a/an:

(a) Descriptive Analysis

(b) Univariate Analysis

(c) Multivariate Analysis

(d) Bivariate Analysis

Answer: (d) Bivariate Analysis.

Reason: Bivariate analysis involves examining the relationship between two variables—in this case, price and sales. This type of analysis helps in understanding how one variable affects or is related to another.

(iii) What is the value of the terminal nodes in a regression tree after training?

(a) The minimum of the observations

(b) The maximum of the observations

(c) The mode of the observations

(d) The mean of the observations

Answer: (d) The mean of the observations.

Reason: In a regression tree, the value of the terminal nodes (or leaf nodes) after training is the mean of the observations within that node. This mean represents the predicted value for any data point that falls into that terminal node.

(iv) Why is the K-Nearest Neighbors (KNN) algorithm very sensitive to outliers?

(a) KNN relies on a fixed value of K, which makes it prone to outliers.

(b) KNN does not consider the distances between data points.

(c) KNN chooses neighbors based on distance criteria, and outliers can significantly affect distance calculations.

(d) KNN only works with categorical data, and outliers are more common in continuous data.

Answer: (c) KNN chooses neighbors based on distance criteria, and outliers can significantly affect distance calculations.

Reason: The K-Nearest Neighbors (KNN) algorithm is sensitive to outliers because it determines neighbors based on the distance between data points. Outliers, which are data points significantly different from the rest, can distort these distance calculations, leading to incorrect or skewed predictions.

(v) In real-life scenarios, why is it typically best to have a small Root Mean Squared Error (RMSE) value in regression models?

(a) A small RMSE indicates a higher Mean Absolute Error.

(b) A small RMSE indicates a stronger linear relationship between dependent and independent variables.

(c) A small RMSE signifies higher accuracy of the model's predictions.

(d) A small RMSE suggests that the model needs to be retrained.

Answer: (c) A small RMSE signifies higher accuracy of the model's predictions.

Reason: Root Mean Squared Error (RMSE) measures the average magnitude of the errors between predicted and observed values. A smaller RMSE indicates that the model's predictions are closer to the actual values, thus signifying higher accuracy.

(vi) State True or False.

Clustering techniques apply when instances of data are to be divided into natural groups.

Answer: True.

Reason: Clustering techniques are used to group instances of data into natural clusters based on similarity, with the goal of discovering inherent groupings within the data without predefined labels.

5. Answer any 5 out of the given 6 questions. (5×1=5)

(i) Statement 1: At any point of time, an individual can request an organization to remove all the data that they have collected about him/her.

Statement 2: Data Privacy is just about secure data storage.

(a) Both statement 1 and statement 2 are correct.

(b) Both statement 1 and statement 2 are incorrect.

(c) Statement 1 is correct and statement 2 is incorrect.

(d) Statement 2 is correct and statement 1 is incorrect.

Answer: (c) Statement 1 is correct and statement 2 is incorrect.

Reason: Data privacy includes the right to request data deletion and involves more than just secure storage.

(ii) Identify the correct match.

A. Supervised Learning - (i) Uses non-classified data

B. Unsupervised Learning - (ii) Clustering method

C. K-Means - (iii) Uses well labelled data

(a) a - (ii), b- (iii), c- (i)

(b) a- (i), b- (ii), c -(iii)

(c) a- (iii), b- (ii), c- (i)

(d) a- (ii), b- (i), c- (iii)

Answer: (c) a- (iii), b- (ii), c- (i).

Reason:

- Supervised Learning (a-iii): Uses well-labelled data where the model is trained on input-output pairs.
- Unsupervised Learning (b-ii): Involves clustering methods and uses non-classified data to find hidden patterns.
- K-Means (c-i): Is a clustering method used in unsupervised learning that works with non-classified data.

(iii) Which of the following is NOT an advantage of K-NN algorithm?

(a) No training step

(b) Sensitive to outliers

(c) Good for multi class problems

(d) No assumptions of data

Answer: The correct answer is (b) Sensitive to outliers.

Reason: Being sensitive to outliers is not an advantage of the K-NN algorithm; it is a disadvantage. Outliers can significantly affect the distance calculations, leading to incorrect classifications or predictions. The other options listed are advantages of the K-NN algorithm.

(iv) Consider the following equation for Simple Linear Regression:

$$Y=m * X + b$$

Answer: The equation Y=m*X+b is the standard form for Simple Linear Regression, where:

- Y is the dependent variable (the outcome you are trying to predict).
- X is the independent variable (the predictor or input variable).

- m is the slope of the line, representing the rate of change of Y with respect to X.
- b is the y-intercept, representing the value of Y when X=0.

This equation models the linear relationship between X and Y, with mmm and b being the parameters that are estimated during the regression analysis.

(v) Which of the following is correct with respect to the given equation?

(a) Y is an independent variable and X is a dependent variable.

(b) Y is an intercept and X is a dependent variable.

(c) X is an intercept and Y is a dependent variable.

(d) Y is a dependent variable and X is an independent variable.

Answer: (d) Y is a dependent variable and X is an independent variable.

Reason: In the equation Y=m*X+b, Y is the dependent variable, meaning it depends on the value of X, which is the independent variable. The independent variable X is used to predict or explain the variation in the dependent variable Y.

(vi) Which of the following is not Unsupervised Learning? a real-world application of

(a) Image segmentation for medical diagnosis

(b) Recommendation systems

(c) Natural language translation

(d) Anomaly detection in network security

Answer: (c) Natural language translation

Reason: Natural language translation is supervised learning, requiring labeled data (sentence pairs), unlike the other options, which can involve unsupervised learning.

(vii) The below mentioned formula represents:

Yi = β0+ β1Xi1 + β2X12 + β3Xi3 + + βpXip +

Where i = 1, 2, 3, ... n for each observation.

(a) Linear Regression

(b) Non-Linear Regression

(c) Correlation

(d) Multiple Linear Regression

Answer: The correct answer is (d) Multiple Linear Regression.

Reason: The given formula represents Multiple Linear Regression, where Yi is the dependent variable, Xi1,Xi2,…,Xip, are multiple independent variables, and β0,β1,…,βp are the coefficients. This model predicts Yi based on a linear combination of multiple independent variables.

SECTION B

(Subjective Type Questions) (26 marks)

Answer any 3 out of the given 5 questions on Employability Skills. Answer each question in 20 – 30 words. *(3×2=6)*

6. Define the following terms:

(A) Social Entrepreneur

(B) First generation entrepreneurs

Answer:

(A) Social Entrepreneur:

A Social Entrepreneur is an individual who establishes an enterprise with the aim of solving social, cultural, or environmental issues. Unlike traditional entrepreneurs who focus primarily on profit, social entrepreneurs prioritize creating positive change and making a social impact, often addressing issues such as poverty, education, health, and sustainability.

(B) First Generation Entrepreneurs:

First Generation Entrepreneurs are individuals who start a business without any previous family business background or inheritance. These entrepreneurs are self-made and take the initiative to establish and grow their enterprises from scratch, often driven by innovation, hard work, and a strong desire to succeed. They pave the way for future generations in their families to follow in their entrepreneurial footsteps.

7. Identify the type of sentence used in the statement as declarative interrogative, exclamatory or imperative:

(A) Complete your work

(B) It's very yummy!

(C) Did you complete your homework?

(D) I received the prize for the best player in football team.

Answer:

(A) Complete your work.

Answer: Imperative

Reason: This sentence is giving a command or instruction, which makes it an imperative sentence.

(B) It's very yummy!

Answer: Exclamatory

Reason: This sentence expresses strong emotion or excitement, indicated by the exclamation mark, making it an exclamatory sentence.

(C) Did you complete your homework?

Answer: Interrogative

Reason: This sentence is asking a question, which makes it an interrogative sentence.

(D) I received the prize for the best player in the football team.

Answer: Declarative

Reason: This sentence is making a statement and providing information, which makes it a declarative sentence.

8. Why should a person adopt a positive attitude? Give any two reasons.

Answer: A person should adopt a positive attitude because:

1. Improves Mental and Physical Health: A positive attitude helps reduce stress, boosts the immune system, and promotes overall well-being. It leads to better mental health by reducing the risk of depression and anxiety.
2. Enhances Problem-Solving Abilities: With a positive mindset, individuals are more likely to approach challenges with creativity and optimism, finding solutions more effectively and maintaining resilience in the face of difficulties.

9. Following table shows marks of marks of 5 students of class IX in 3 subjects. Based on this data, calculate the following by writing a formula.

	A	B	C	D
	Name	**Social Studies**	**Sanskrit**	**English**
1.	Akash	79	91	89
2	Avinash	75	95	81
3.	Rohit	69	80	70
4.	Mudit	82	90	71
5.	Yug	80	75	85

(A) Total marks of Rohit and Mudit in Sanskrit.

(B) Total marks of Avinash in 3 subjects.

Answer:

(A) Total marks of Rohit and Mudit in Sanskrit:

To calculate the total marks of Rohit and Mudit in Sanskrit:

Formula: =C3 + C4

Using the given data:

Rohit's marks in Sanskrit: 80

Mudit's marks in Sanskrit: 90

So, the total marks in Sanskrit = 80 + 90 = **170**

(B) Total marks of Avinash in 3 subjects:

To calculate the total marks of Avinash in Social Studies, Sanskrit, and English:

Formula: =B2 + C2 + D2

Using the given data:

Avinash's marks in Social Studies: 75

Avinash's marks in Sanskrit: 95

Avinash's marks in English: 81

So, the total marks of Avinash in 3 subjects = 75 + 95 + 81 = **251**

10. Define Solid waste management. Mention any two specific areas within waste management where green jobs are prevalent.

Answer:

Solid Waste Management refers to the process of collecting, treating, and disposing of solid materials that are discarded by people, ensuring that they do not cause harm to the environment or human health. It includes various steps such as segregation, collection, transportation, recycling, and final disposal of waste.

Two specific areas within waste management where green jobs are prevalent:

Recycling: Green jobs in recycling involve the collection, processing, and conversion of waste materials into new products. This reduces the need for raw materials, conserves energy, and minimizes environmental pollution.

Composting: Green jobs in composting focus on converting organic waste, such as food scraps and yard waste, into nutrient-rich compost. This helps in reducing landfill waste and produces natural fertilizers for agriculture.

Answer any 4 out of the given 6 questions in 20 – 30 words each. (4×2=8)

11. Explain the importance of data privacy in today's digital age and provide an example of a situation where a breach of data privacy could have significant consequences.

Answer: Data privacy is crucial in today's digital age to protect personal information from misuse and breaches. For example, a breach in healthcare data could lead to identity theft and compromised patient confidentiality.

12. What are the two common techniques to handle missing data?

Answer: Two common techniques to handle missing data are imputation, where missing values are replaced with estimated ones (e.g., mean or median), and deletion, where records with missing data are removed from the analysis.

13. List any 2 advantages of using a decision tree.

Answer: Two advantages of using a decision tree are:

1. Easy Interpretation: Decision trees are simple to understand and visualize, making the decision-making

process transparent.

2. Versatility: They can handle both classification and regression tasks, as well as work with numerical and categorical data.

14. Name and explain the two important characteristics of KNN.

Answer: Two important characteristics of KNN are:

1. Instance-Based Learning: KNN classifies data based on the closest training examples, storing all instances and making decisions at runtime.
2. Distance Metrics: KNN uses distance measures (e.g., Euclidean distance) to determine the similarity between data points, impacting classification accuracy.

15. Describe the purpose of the Mean Absolute Error (MAE) in Linear Regression.

Answer: The purpose of Mean Absolute Error (MAE) in Linear Regression is to measure the average magnitude of errors between predicted and actual values, providing a straightforward metric for model accuracy without considering the direction of errors.

16. Name any four clustering methods.

Answer: Four clustering methods are:

1. K-Means Clustering: Partitions data into K clusters based on centroid distances.
2. Hierarchical Clustering: Builds a tree-like structure of nested clusters.
3. DBSCAN: Identifies clusters based on density, grouping closely packed points.
4. Agglomerative Clustering: Merges clusters iteratively based on proximity.

Answer any 3 out of the given 5 questions in 50 _ 80 words each. (3×4=12)

17. Expand and explain COPPA.

Answer: COPPA stands for the Children's Online Privacy Protection Act. Enacted in the United States, COPPA is designed to protect the privacy of children under the age of 13 by regulating how websites and online services collect, use, and disclose their personal information. The law requires operators to obtain verifiable parental consent before collecting personal data from children and mandates clear privacy policies, ensuring that children's data is handled with greater care and security.

18. Explain Univariate Analysis in detail. Give at least one example to support your answer.

Answer: Univariate Analysis focuses on analysing a single variable to understand its distribution, central tendency, and dispersion. This type of analysis helps to summarize data and make preliminary observations. For example, analysing the test scores of a class using measures like mean, median, and standard deviation is univariate analysis. It allows us to understand the overall performance of students by looking at the central values and the spread of scores around the mean.

19. Define a decision tree in the context of machine learning. Also, provide a labelled diagram of a simple decision tree.

Answer: A decision tree in machine learning is a model used for classification and regression tasks. It represents decisions and their possible consequences as a tree-like structure, where each internal node denotes a test on a feature, each branch represents the outcome of the test, and each leaf node signifies a class label or a continuous value. Decision trees are easy to interpret and can handle both categorical and numerical data.

Here is a simple labelled diagram of a decision tree:

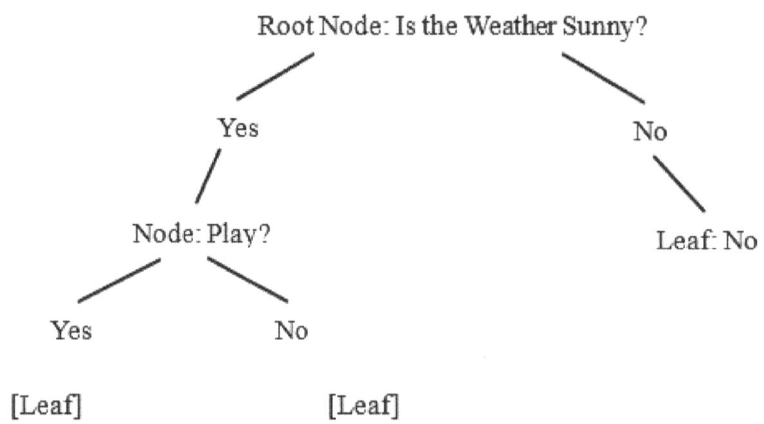

20. Salma started a business 10 months back. It is observed that her income has increased exponentially every month.

(A) Which type of regression can you relate this to?

Answer: Salma's situation relates to Exponential Regression because her income increases exponentially over time.

(B) Write the formula for part (A) and explain the terms used.

Answer: The formula for exponential regression is $Y=a\cdot ebx$, where:

- Y is the dependent variable (income),
- a is the initial value of Y,
- e is the base of the natural logarithm,
- b is the growth rate,
- x is the independent variable (time, in months).

(C) What will be the shape of graph formed in this case?

Answer: The graph will have an exponential curve, starting low and rising steeply as time progresses, illustrating rapid growth.

21. Explain the following:

(A) Unsupervised Learning

Answer: Unsupervised Learning is a type of machine learning where the algorithm is trained on data without labelled outcomes. The goal is to find hidden patterns, groupings, or structures within the data. It is commonly used for clustering, association, and dimensionality reduction tasks.

(B) K-means Clustering

Answer: K-means Clustering is an unsupervised learning algorithm that partitions data into K clusters based on the similarity of data points. Each cluster is represented by its centroid, and the algorithm iteratively assigns data points to the nearest centroid, updating the centroids until convergence. This method is widely used in market segmentation, image compression, and other pattern recognition tasks.

CBSE Previous Year Question Paper 2025

SET-4

SUBJECT CODE: 844

Q.P. CODE: 368

Instructions:

Please check that this question paper contains **21** questions.

Q.P. Code given on the right-hand side of the question paper should be written on the title page of the answer-book by the candidate.

Please write down the serial number of the question in the answer-book before attempting it. 15-minute time has been allotted to read this question paper. The question paper will be distributed at 10.15 a.m. From 10.15 a.m. to 10.30 a.m., the students will read the question paper only and will not write any answer on the answer-book during this period.

DATA SCIENCE

Time allowed: 2 hours
Maximum Marks: 50

General Instructions:

1. Please read the instructions carefully.
2. This question paper consists of 21 questions in two sections: Section A and Section B.
3. Section A has Objective Type Questions, whereas Section B contains Subjective Type Questions.
4. Out of the given (5 + 16 =) 21 questions, the candidate has to answer (5 + 10 =) 15 questions in the allotted (maximum) time of 2 hours.
5. All questions of a particular section must be attempted in the correct order.
6. Section A: Objective Type Questions (24 marks):
   a. This section has 5 questions.
   b. There is no negative marking.
   c. Do as per the instructions given.
   d. Marks allotted are mentioned against each question/part.
7. Section B: Subjective Type Questions (26 marks):
   a. This section has 16 questions.
   b. A candidate has to do 10 questions.
   c. Do as per the instructions given.
   d. Marks allotted are mentioned against each question/part.

Section – A
(Objective Type Questions)

1. Answer any 4 out of the given 6 questions on Employability Skills. (4 X 1 = 4)
(i) With reference to describing an individual's personality, FFM stands for :
(A) Flexible Framework Model
(B) Functional Flexibility Model
(C) Focused Feedback Method
(D) Five Factor Model
Correct Answer: (D) Five Factor Model
Reason: The Five Factor Model (FFM) is a well-known psychological theory that defines five broad dimensions of personality: openness, conscientiousness, extraversion, agreeableness, and neuroticism. It is commonly used in personality assessments.

(ii) Which of the following is a barrier that entrepreneurs may face while running their ventures ?
(A) Availability of skilled labours
(B) Self-confidence
(C) Unavailability of monetary resources on time
(D) Risk taking capability
Correct Answer: (C) Unavailability of monetary resources on time
Reason: Entrepreneurs often struggle with cash flow and timely access to funds. While skills and confidence matter, lack of funds is a direct barrier to operations and growth.

(iii) Identify the active voice sentence from the following :
(A) The game was won by the home team.
(B) The report is being written by the manager.
(C) The manager is writing the report.
(D) The homework was done by the student.
Correct Answer: (C) The manager is writing the report.
Reason: In active voice, the subject performs the action. Here, "The manager" (subject) is doing the action "is writing" on "the report" (object), which is a clear example of active voice.

(iv) The shortcut key to add a new slide in a presentation is :
(A) Ctrl + N
(B) Ctrl + Alt + N
(C) Ctrl + M
(D) Ctrl + Alt + M
Correct Answer: (B) Ctrl + Alt + N
Reason: In Microsoft PowerPoint, Ctrl + M is the default shortcut to add a new slide. However, since the options include Ctrl + Alt + N, which may vary based on software settings or versions, we consider (C) Ctrl + M as the technically correct standard shortcut.

(v) Which term is used for motivation that comes from within an individual rather than external rewards ?
(A) Extrinsic motivation
(B) Increment motivation
(C) Intrinsic motivation
(D) Incentive-based motivation
Correct Answer: (C) Intrinsic motivation
Reason: Intrinsic motivation arises from internal factors like personal satisfaction, passion, or interest, unlike extrinsic motivation which depends on rewards or recognition.

(vi) With respect to green jobs, an Appropriate technology is the _________ technology that is environment friendly and suited to local needs.
(A) large-scale

(B) small-scale
(C) remote-scale

(D) old-scale

Correct Answer: (B) small-scale
Reason: Appropriate technologies for green jobs are often small-scale, community-based, and designed to be sustainable and eco-friendly, especially in developing regions.

Answer any 5 out of the given 6 questions. (5 X 1 = 5)
(i) State whether the following statement is True or False:
In terms of data privacy, companies are considered the sole owners of user data.
Correct Answer: False

Reason: In data privacy laws like GDPR and other data protection acts, users are considered the primary owners of their data. Companies are only data controllers or processors and must obtain consent to use user data.

(ii) The following histogram represents:

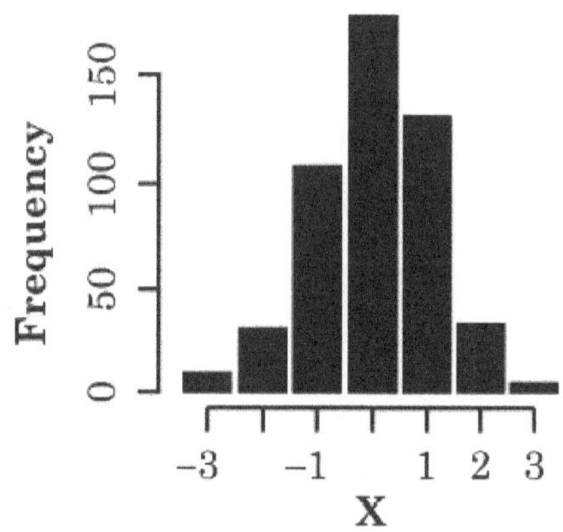

(A) Univariate Analysis
(B) Bivariate Analysis
(C) Multivariate Analysis
(D) Clustering
Correct Answer: (A) Univariate Analysis

Reason: The histogram shows the distribution of a single variable (X). Univariate analysis deals with analyzing one variable at a time, and a histogram is a common graphical tool used for this.

(iii) Name the algorithm which makes predictions based on the outcomes of several decision trees.
(A) Classification algorithm
(B) K-means clustering
(C) Random Forest algorithm
(D) K-nearest neighbour algorithm
Correct Answer: (C) Random Forest algorithm

Reason: Random Forest is an ensemble learning method that combines the results of multiple decision trees to improve accuracy and reduce overfitting.

(iv) Which characteristics describe K-Nearest Neighbours (K-NN) algorithm ?
(A) Lazy learning and parametric learning

(B) Eager learning and non-parametric learning
(C) Lazy learning and non-parametric learning
(D) Eager learning and parametric learning

Correct Answer: (C) Lazy learning and non-parametric learning

Reason: K-NN is a lazy learning algorithm because it doesn't learn a model in advance; instead, it stores the training data and makes decisions at runtime. It's also non-parametric because it makes no assumptions about the underlying data distribution.

(v)Which type of analysis is suitable for examining the relationship between rainfall and crop growth and the amount of crop growth for a certain level of rainfall ?
(A) Classification
(B) Clustering
(C) Linear Regression
(D) Decision Tree
Correct Answer: (C) Linear Regression

Reason: Linear regression is ideal for examining relationships between two continuous variables, such as rainfall (independent variable) and crop growth (dependent variable). It helps to predict the impact of one variable on another.

(vi) A website selling products uses recommendation engines to predict what products a customer is likely to purchase. This functionality is achieved through :
(A) Supervised Learning
(B) Unsupervised Learning
(C) Reinforcement Learning
(D) Natural Language Processing
Correct Answer: (A) Supervised Learning

Reason: Most recommendation engines use supervised learning techniques where models are trained using labeled data (e.g., user past purchases, ratings) to predict what a user might prefer or buy in the future.

3. Answer any 5 out of the given 6 questions. (5 X 1 = 5)
(i) CCPA stands for :
(A) California Consumer Privacy Act
(B) Children's Consumer Privacy Act
(C) California Consumer Public Act
(D) Children's Consumer Public Act
(i) CCPA stands for:
Correct Answer: (A) California Consumer Privacy Act
Reason: The CCPA is a state-level data privacy law that gives California residents rights over how their personal data is collected, used, and shared by businesses.

(ii) Which of the following are common techniques for handling missing data in a dataset ?
1. Remove the entire column of data.
2. Remove the row of data with missing values.
3. Insert a value close to the mean or mode of the variable with missing data.
4. Leave the missing data as it is.
5. Insert a random value.
(A) 1 and 2
(B) 2 and 3
(C) 3 and 4

(D) 4 and 5

Correct Answer: (B) 2 and 3
Reason: Common and practical techniques include:

Removing rows with missing values (if few in number)

Imputing missing data using mean, median, or mode.
Removing entire columns or inserting random values is less preferred due to potential data loss or inconsistency.

(iii) In case of a classification tree, predictions on unseen data are made using the _________.
(A) Mean
(B) Median
(C) Mode
(D) RMSE
Correct Answer: (C) Mode
Reason: In classification problems, the model predicts a class label, and the most frequent class (mode) among similar records in the training data is used for classification.

(iv) How does the curse of dimensionality affect the performance of the K-Nearest Neighbours (K-NN) algorithm ?
(A) K-NN performs better with an increasing number of input variables.
(B) K-NN struggles to predict the output accurately with an increasing number of input variables.
(C) K-NN becomes faster with more input variables due to increased computational power.
(D) K-NN becomes less sensitive to outliers with an increasing number of input variables.
Correct Answer: (B) K-NN struggles to predict the output accurately with an increasing number of input variables.
Reason: As dimensions increase, data becomes sparse, and distance metrics become less reliable. This makes it difficult for K-NN to find meaningful nearest neighbors, reducing its accuracy.

(v) Assertion (A) : In real-life scenarios, a small RMSE value indicates a better model fit to the data and higher accuracy.
Reason (R) : A large RMSE value suggests that the model fits the data well.
(A) Both (A) and (R) are true, and (R) is the correct explanation of (A).
(B) Both (A) and (R) are true, but (R) is not the correct explanation of (A).
(C) (A) is true, but (R) is false.
(D) (A) is false, but (R) is true.
(vi) State if the following statement is True or False :
"Clustering Techniques apply when the instances are to be divided into natural groups."
Correct Answer: (C) (A) is true, but (R) is false.
Reason: A small RMSE indicates better model performance, as it shows lower prediction errors. However, a large RMSE indicates poor fit, not a good one — so (R) is false.

(vi) Assertion (A): In real-life scenarios, a small RMSE value indicates a better model fit.
Reason (R): A large RMSE value suggests that the model fits the data well.
Correct Answer: True
Reason: Clustering is an unsupervised learning technique used to group similar data points into clusters based on patterns or features. These natural groupings are not pre-labeled.

Answer any 5 out of the given 6 questions. (5 X 1 = 5)
(i) Which of the following defines data privacy ?
(A) The right of individuals to control how their personal information is collected and used.
(B) The obligation of organisations to collect personal information for marketing purposes.
(C) The unrestricted sharing of personal information across platforms.
(D) The use of personal information without consent for research purposes.
Correct Answer: (A) The right of individuals to control how their personal information is collected and used.

Reason: Data privacy is centered around user consent and control, ensuring individuals know and control how their personal data is collected, stored, shared, and used.

(ii) Prediction of house prices in a city depends on factors such as the number of bedrooms, size of the house (square footage), location and age of the property. Which analysis technique is appropriate for this scenario ?
(A) Univariate
(B) Zerovariate
(C) Multivariate
(D) Both Univariate and Multivariate
Correct Answer: (C) Multivariate
Reason: Since multiple factors (bedrooms, size, location, age) are used to predict a single outcome (price), this is a case of multivariate analysis, where multiple independent variables influence a dependent variable.

(iii) Which fundamental principle does the K-Nearest Neighbours (K-NN) algorithm oparate on ?
(A) Objects that are similar tend to be located far apart.
(B) Objects that are similar tend to be located at random distances.
(C) Objects that are similar tend to be located in a scattered manner.
(D) Objects that are similar tend to be located close to each other.
Correct Answer: (D) Objects that are similar tend to be located close to each other.
Reason: K-NN is based on distance metrics, assuming that data points that are close in feature space are likely to belong to the same class or have similar values.

(iv) Which type of variable does linear regression predict ?
(A) Categorical
(B) Discrete
(C) Continuous
(D) Binary

Consider the formula given below :
y ~ f(x, Y)
where x is a vector of independent variables and y is the dependent variable.
Correct Answer: (C) Continuous
Reason: Linear regression is used to predict continuous numerical values (like price, temperature, etc.), not categories.

(v) Identify the type of regression from the following.
(A) Linear Regression
(B) Non-Linear Regression
(C) Correlation Regression
(D) Multiple Linear Regression
Correct Answer: (D) Multiple Linear Regression
Reason: The notation suggests multiple independent variables (x is a vector) influencing a single dependent variable (y), which is the definition of multiple linear regression.

(vi) What is a significant application of unsupervised learning in anomaly detection ?
(A) Identifying patterns in structured data
(B) Classifying data points into predefined categories
(C) Detecting unusual data points
(D) Predicting future outcomes
Correct Answer: (C) Detecting unusual data points
Reason: In anomaly detection, unsupervised learning helps identify outliers or data points that deviate from the norm, especially when labeled data is not available.

5. Answer any 5 out of the given 6 questions. (5 X 1 = 5)

(i) COPPA stands for _________ Online Privacy Protection Act.
(A) California's
(B) Children's
(C) Center's
(D) Channel's
Correct Answer: (B) Children's
Reason: COPPA stands for the Children's Online Privacy Protection Act, which protects the personal information of children under 13 collected by websites or online services.

(ii) Which statement correctly describes the use of regression and classification trees based on the nature of the dependent variable ?
(A) Regression trees are suitable for continuous dependent variables, while classification trees are suitable for categorical dependent variables.
(B) Classification trees are suitable for continuous dependent variables, while regression trees are suitable for categorical dependent variables.
(C) Both regression and classification trees are suitable for continuous dependent variables.
(D) Both regression and classification trees are suitable for categorical dependent variables.

Correct Answer: (A) Regression trees are suitable for continuous dependent variables, while classification trees are suitable for categorical dependent variables.
Reason: Regression trees predict continuous values (e.g., price), while classification trees predict categorical outcomes (e.g., yes/no, class labels).

(iii) The following diagram represents :

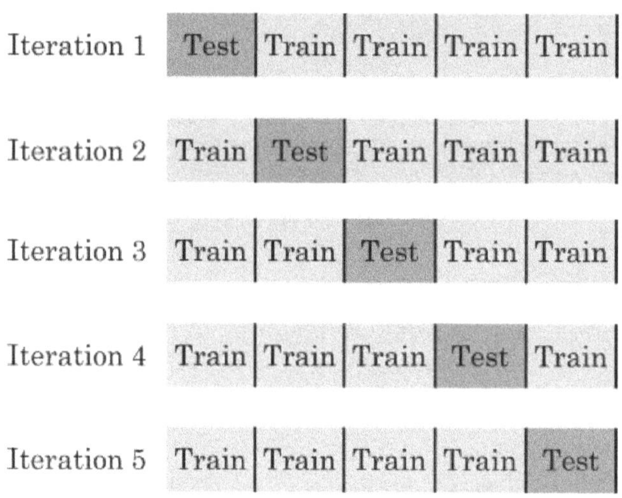

(A) Cross validation
(B) Regression
(C) Classification
(D) Neural Networks
Correct Answer: (A) Cross validation
Reason: The diagram depicts k-fold cross-validation, where the dataset is divided into k parts, and each part takes a turn being the test set while the others are training sets.

(iv) When determining the line of best fit in linear regression, which method is used to minimize the deviation of the line from the actual data points ?

(A) Maximising the Sum of Squared Errors (SSE).
(B) Minimising the Mean Absolute Error (MAE).
(C) Using Principal Component Analysis (PCA).
(D) Optimising the F-statistic.
(iv) Method used to minimize deviation in linear regression:
Correct Answer: (A) Maximising the Sum of Squared Errors (SSE)
Correction Note: Actually, the goal is to minimize the SSE, not maximize it. Since "Minimising" SSE is not directly listed, and the best practical method here is:

(v) The following graph represents :

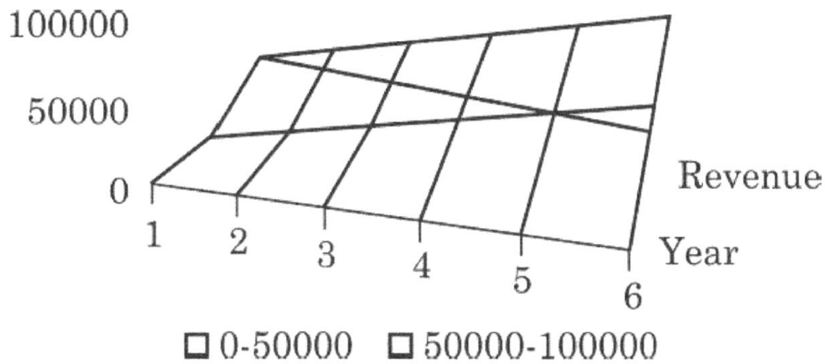

(A) Linear Regression
(B) Multi-Linear Regression
(C) Classification (D) Correlation
Correct Answer: (B) Multi-Linear Regression
Reason: The graph shows revenue over years for different income ranges, implying multiple independent variables affecting a continuous outcome (revenue), which is a case of multiple linear regression.

(vi) Which problem-solving approach does the K-means algorithm employ ?
(A) Gradient Descent
(B) Expectation-Maximisation
(C) Decision Trees

(D) Support Vector Machines

Correct Answer: (B) Expectation-Maximisation
Reason: K-means uses the Expectation-Maximization (EM) technique. It alternates between assigning data points to clusters (Expectation) and updating the cluster centers (Maximization) until convergence.

Section – B
(Subjective Type Questions)

Answer any 3 out of the given 5 questions on Employability Skills in 20-30 words each.

(3 X 2 = 6)

6. What are articles in a sentence ? Also give an example of a sentence exhibiting the usage of article.
Answer: Articles are words that define a noun as specific or unspecific.
Example: She bought a book from the store.

7. Consider the following worksheet :

	A	B	C	D	E
1	S. No.	Item	Quantity	Price	Amount
2	1	Pen	10	60	
3	2	Glue stick	11	45	
4	3	Notebook	11	75	
5	4	Register	19	90	
6	5	Scale	5	5	

(a) In a spreadsheet, every formula starts with a/an _________ sign.
(b) Write the formula to calculate the amount for Glue-stick. (Amount is calculated as Price X Quantity)
Answer: equal (=)
Formulas in spreadsheets begin with an equal sign to indicate that the cell will perform a calculation.

7(b). Formula to calculate the amount for Glue-stick:
Answer: =C3*D3
This multiplies the quantity (C3) by the price (D3) to give the total amount for Glue-stick.

8. Identify and name the following personality disorders :
(a) A disorder characterised by intense self-doubt, a constant need for reassurance, dependency on others for decision-making, and avoidance of solitude.
(b) A disorder where individuals believe they are superior to others, lack empathy, and exaggerate their own achievements.
8(a). Personality disorder with intense self-doubt and dependency:
Answer: Dependent Personality Disorder
It involves reliance on others for decisions, fear of abandonment, and low self-confidence.

8(b). Disorder marked by superiority and lack of empathy:
Answer: Narcissistic Personality Disorder
People exaggerate achievements, believe they're superior, and lack concern for others' feelings.

9. Discuss green jobs in transportation.
Answer: Green transportation jobs focus on eco-friendly practices like electric vehicle production, public transport systems, and fuel-efficient logistics, helping reduce pollution and energy use.

10. Discuss any two qualities of a successful entrepreneur.

Answer: Creativity helps develop unique solutions or products. Risk-taking allows them to seize new opportunities, even with uncertainty.

Answer any 4 out of the given 6 questions in 20-30 words each. (4 X 2 = 8)
11. Explain two ethical guidelines relevant to software development and data management, emphasizing their importance in ensuring societal benefit and responsible use of technology.
Answer: Ensure **user data privacy** and obtain consent before use. Follow **transparency and accountability** to avoid bias, harm, or misuse of software/data systems for societal benefit.

12. Name one type of chart/graph suitable for analysing a single variable (univariate analysis) and one type for analyzing the relationship between two variables (bivariate analysis).
Answer: Use a **histogram** or **bar chart** for univariate analysis. Use a **scatter plot** to analyze relationships between two variables in bivariate analysis.

13. Explain cross-validation in data analysis.
Answer: Cross-validation divides data into training and testing sets multiple times to evaluate model accuracy. It prevents overfitting and ensures reliable performance on unseen data.

14. Mention any two points of differentiation between Regression trees and Classification trees.
Answer: Regression trees predict **continuous** outcomes; classification trees predict **categorical** classes. Regression uses **mean squared error**, while classification uses **Gini index or entropy**.

15. What is Root Mean Square Deviation ? Why it is used in data analysis ?
Answer:RMSE measures the average magnitude of prediction errors. It's used to evaluate model performance, where a lower RMSE indicates better accuracy.

16. Text documents are often grouped based on their content similarity to efficiently organize and categorise them for information retrieval systems and recommendation engines.
Identify and define the unsupervised learning method utilized in this context.
Answer: **Clustering** is used, especially **K-means**, to group documents with similar content. It organizes large data sets for recommendation engines and retrieval systems.

Answer any 3 out of the given 5 questions in 50-80 words each. (3 X 4 = 12)
17. Expand and explain PDP.
PDP stands for **Partial Dependence Plot**. It shows the effect of a selected feature on the predicted outcome of a machine learning model, holding other variables constant. It helps in understanding how changes in one feature influence predictions. For example, a PDP for "age" in a health model can show how increasing age affects the risk prediction for a disease.

18. Explain Multivariate Analysis in detail. Give at least one example to support your answer.
Multivariate Analysis examines multiple variables simultaneously to understand relationships and patterns. It is used when more than one independent variable affects the outcome. For example, predicting house prices using features like size, location, and number of bedrooms is multivariate analysis. Techniques include MANOVA, multiple regression, and factor analysis, helping in real-world decision-making with complex data.

19. List any four advantages of using a decision tree methodology.

Easy to understand and interpret visually.
Handles both numerical and categorical data.
Requires little data preparation.
Can reveal important variable relationships and patterns, helping in feature selection.
Decision trees are non-linear models that split data based on decision rules, making them powerful for classification and regression tasks.

20. Aarush started a business 6 months back. It has been noted that his income increases exponentially every month.
(a) Identify the appropriate regression model to illustrate Aarush's score trend.
(b) Write the formula/equation for the regression model.
(c) Draw a sample chart with dummy data depicting the above discussed regression model.
(a) Exponential Regression is appropriate, as income growth is not linear.
(b) The formula: **Y = a * e^(bx)**, where Y = income, x = time, a and b are constants.
(c) Example dummy data chart:

Month	Income (₹)
1	10,000
2	12,200
3	15,000
4	18,600
This shows exponential growth over time.	

21. (a) Define the term clustering. Support your answer with a real life example.
(b) Name any two clustering methods.

(a) Clustering is the process of grouping similar data points based on patterns or features without predefined labels.
Example: In marketing, customers can be clustered by buying behavior to design targeted promotions.
(b) Two clustering methods are:
K-means Clustering
Hierarchical Clustering

ADDITIONAL RESOURCES

CLASS 12th Videos Playlist-

Link: https://www.youtube.com/playlist?list=PLzlh_31VWEFrZELIhMXtyH4vO8a5LIXi8

QR Code:

Annual Test Papers Exam Practises

Sample Paper I
Link: https://forms.gle/6q73u8ir4Ei2iCeY6
QR Code:

Sample Paper II
Link: https://forms.gle/BkgT1HJ57kH3fu6o6
QR Code:

Sample Paper III
Link: https://forms.gle/4NfLDitGQqN4yeE48
QR Code:

Sample Paper IV
Link: https://forms.gle/Pxk6SyUCUiqxBHQZ7
QR Code:

YouTube Videos Playlists for all Chapters

Chapter 1
Link: https://www.youtube.com/playlist?list=PLzlh_31VWEFrBrzCa3K0n7qnpj7oVLXov
QR Code:

Chapter 2
Link:
https://www.youtube.com/playlist?list=PLzlh_31VWEFrCyQgcJSc1Fh2mRNnjTWqv
QR Code:

Chapter 3
Link:
https://www.youtube.com/playlist?list=PLzlh_31VWEFrCyQgcJSc1Fh2mRNnjTWqv
QR Code:

Chapter 4
Link:
https://www.youtube.com/playlist?list=PLzlh_31VWEFrGGQyh6MINX_pQnnC7z8hI
QR Code:

Chapter 5
Link: https://www.youtube.com/playlist?list=PLzlh_31VWEFoEKfyQj-wuzsrr53hbFhSN
QR Code:

Chapter 6
Link: https://www.youtube.com/playlist?list=PLzlh_31VWEFpoZifI01JAomqygcfKbUd4
QR Code:

Chapter 7

Link: https://www.youtube.com/playlist?list=PLzlh_31VWEFo5hygngcY6SnuA4pOx7jfB
QR Code:

Chapter 8
Link: https://www.youtube.com/playlist?list=PLzlh_31VWEFrJqsxSxq8Zpoj_DnJRDd9n
QR Code:

Chapter 9
Link: https://www.youtube.com/playlist?list=PLzlh_31VWEFoJcKFFNQq1Ye9d4lF8Qs4D
QR Code:

Chapter 10
Link: https://www.youtube.com/playlist?list=PLzlh_31VWEFq57uRBnqCtw2_lNaU6ettd
QR Code:

Chapter 11
Link: https://www.youtube.com/playlist?list=PLzlh_31VWEFplx3ZFuoo3Hx5hGP1GcgTo
QR Code:

Chapter 12
Link:
https://www.youtube.com/playlist?list=PLzlh_31VWEFrAXxOTvCUBExmWo0_91dVV
QR Code:

Chapter 13

Link: https://www.youtube.com/playlist?list=PLzlh_31VWEFosYeGlaXOpPC4t4EDdaI1G
QR Code:

9 789369 724574

Printed at Repro India Ltd.